SANTA MONICA
PUBLIC
LIBRARY

www.smpl.org

4-WEEK LOAN

TELEPHONE RENEWALS:
Main Library. 451-1866
Ocean Park Branch 392-3804
Fairview Branch 450-0443
Montana Branch 829-7081

DATE DUE

A BLUE BANNER BIOGRAPHY

Alicia Keys

By John Bankston

P.O. Box 196
Hockessin, Delaware 19707
Visit us on the web: www.mitchelllane.com
Comments? email us: mitchelllane@mitchelllane.com

Printing   1   2   3   4   5   6   7   8   9

Blue Banner Biographies

Alicia Keys	Allen Iverson	Avril Lavigne
Beyoncé	Bow Wow	Britney Spears
Christina Aguilera	Christopher Paul Curtis	Clay Aiken
Condoleezza Rice	Daniel Radcliffe	Derek Jeter
Eminem	Eve	Ja Rule
Jay-Z	Jennifer Lopez	J. K. Rowling
Jodie Foster	Lance Armstrong	Mary-Kate and Ashley Olsen
Melissa Gilbert	Michael Jackson	Missy Elliott
Nelly	P. Diddy	Queen Latifah
Rita Williams-Garcia	Ritchie Valens	Ron Howard
Rudy Giuliani	Sally Field	Selena
Shirley Temple		

Library of Congress Cataloging-in-Publication Data
Bankston, John, 1974–
    Alicia Keys / John Bankston
        p. cm. -- (A blue banner biography)
    Includes bibliographical references and index.
    Discography: p.
    ISBN 1-58415-327-X (library bound)
    1. Keys, Alicia—Juvenile literature. 2. Singers—United States—Biography—Juvenile literature.
I. Title. II. Series.
ML3930.K39B361 2004
782.42164'092—dc22

                                                                                                    2004021873

ABOUT THE AUTHOR: Born in Boston, Massachussetts, **John Bankston** began publishing articles in newspapers and magazines while still a teenager. Since then, he has written over two hundred articles, and contributed chapters to books such as *Crimes of Passion,* and *Death Row 2000,* which have been sold in bookstores across the world. He has written numerous biographies for young adults, including Mandy Moore and Alexander Fleming and the Story of Penicillin (Mitchell Lane). He currently lives in Portland, Oregon.

PHOTO CREDITS: Cover—Frank Micelotta/Getty Images; p. 4—INSA KORTH/AFP/Getty Images; p. 10—Fitzroy Barrett/Globe Photos; p. 12—Tim Shaffer/Reuters; p. 16—Gary Hershorn/Reuters; p. 20—Fashion Wire Daily; p. 23—Kevin Winter/Getty Images; p. 25—Frank Micelotta/Getty Images; p. 27—Alberto Tamargo/Getty Images.

CONTENTS

Alicia performs at a concert during her Germany tour in Hamburg.

Hell's Kitchen

*H*arlem can be a difficult neighborhood. Located in upper Manhattan, this historic African American community now boasts a diverse population of recent immigrants, Asians, and Latinos. It also has more than its fair share of poverty and crime. There have been few areas the size of Harlem that have contributed so much to the arts—especially literature and music.

In the 1920s and '30s, Harlem went through a Renaissance, a period when its artistic, cultural, and social life peaked. Authors like Langston Hughes and Zora Neale Hurston wrote about the lives of African Americans from their homes in the community near 125th Street. Hot spots like the Cotton Club and the Apollo gained international reputations presenting talents like Billie Holliday and Duke Ellington.

Although the mid- to late-twentieth-century saw the neighborhood's decline, many believe Harlem is now in the middle of its second Renaissance. The old Apollo underwent a renovation in the 1980s and continues to attract well-known performers. Former President Bill Clinton now rents office space in the neighborhood. One of the top musical voices in the early twenty-first century drew her inspiration from its streets.

Alicia Keys was born Alicia Augello Cook on January 25, 1981 in New York City. Although Harlem played a big role in her life's experience, she spent her childhood at 43rd Street and 10th Avenue in an area now called Clinton.

Although Harlem played a big role in her life's experience, she spent her childhood at 43rd Street and 10th Avenue in an area now called Clinton.

Back then it was known as Hell's Kitchen. The neighborhood lived up to the name. Its residents were mainly working class people, and every day they had to weed through streets populated by criminals.

"It was one block from heaven and one block from hell," Alicia told the *Los Angeles Times.*

The daughter of an Italian Irish mother and an African American father, Alicia explained to *The Guardian*, "My mixed race background made me a broad person, able to relate to different cultures. But any woman of color, even a mixed color, is seen as black in America. So, that's how I regard myself."

Her father, Craig Cook, was a flight attendant who left the family when Alicia was still a toddler. Growing up as an only child, Alicia was raised by a struggling single mother. Although the environment in her neighborhood was not the best place to raise a child, Alicia's mom Terri worked hard to bring her daughter up the right way.

Terri worked as a part time actress and a paralegal, but she spent any free time she had encouraging her daughter to pursue a variety of creative pursuits.

As a child, Alicia developed her talents as a dancer, artist, gymnast, and actress. In kindergarten, she won the lead role of Dorothy in a school production of the *Wizard of Oz*, but the area where young Alicia excelled the most was in music. A small piano divided Alicia's room from the living area, and at age seven she learned how to play. She quickly progressed from Chopsticks to Mozart and Chopin, whom she jokingly calls, "My dawg."

> *As a child, Alicia developed her talents as a dancer, artist, gymnast, and actress.*

Even as a kid, Alicia knew music was in her heart, and she recognized that it could mean a future career. Fortunately, Alicia was a child of New York City, a place offering everything from free concerts in Central Park to the background music of street and subway performers. She had the chance to take advantage of the culture the city provided.

It also offered an educational opportunity.

The Professional Performing Arts School has been guiding young actors, singers, dancers, and musicians for decades. During the 1980s, the school was one of the inspirations for the popular movie and television series, *Fame*. In 1993, at 12 years old, Alicia auditioned for the school. It was a very competitive process, because there are always many more students trying out than there are spots available at the public school.

The staff recognized Alicia's potential and admitted her to the school. She was in, and she was on her way.

In 1993, at 12 years old, Alicia auditioned for the [Professional Performing Arts] school. It was a very competitive process . . .

EmBishion

*F*or someone as creative as Alicia, the Professional Performing Arts School was an artistic playground. She took classes in everything from dance to theater. When her classical piano teacher admitted there was nothing left for him to teach her, Alicia switched to jazz. She studied legends like Miles Davis, Duke Ellington, and Billie Holliday, along with 1960s singers like Stevie Wonder and Carole King. But for 13 year old Alicia, no one else inspired her as much as Marvin Gaye and his breakthrough album *What's Going On*.

"It just hit me like a rock over the head," Alicia admitted to the *New York Times*. "I had never heard a body of music like that, so in tune with people and reality and consciousness, socially and politically and in love with stillness and then turmoil. It was like

Alicia was inspired by many musicians, but her idol is Marvin Gaye.

everything that you have felt at one point or another, all in one, bam!"

Alicia drew on Marvin Gaye's work as she began to craft her own songs, "The Life" and "Butterflyz," which she would later sing on her album. As she traveled regularly between her Clinton home and school in Harlem, she formed friendships with two other young women who were as inspired by then popular girl group En Vogue as Alicia was by Marvin Gaye. The three girls formed a group called EmBishion and began working in small New York City venues. Singing as a trio was difficult for Alicia because the girls could never agree on what songs to perform.

It was Alicia's own musical strengths that got her noticed. During a performance by EmBishion at the Police Athletic League on 124th Street, a vocal coach named Conrad Robinson noticed Alicia's talents. He worked with her to help improve her voice and then contacted his brother Jeff.

Jeff managed singers.

"She sang Mary J. Blige, and I was like, 'OK, she's got soul,' " Jeff Robinson told the *Metro*, recalling the first time he heard Alicia. "But then she sat down at the piano and started playing Scott Joplin and I was like, 'Whoa!' "

Jeff signed the teen to a management agreement, which meant that he would earn 15 percent of anything she made as a singer. In the beginning that was 15 percent of not much money. Instead of pushing

> *Singing as a trio was difficult for Alicia because the girls could never agree on what songs to perform.*

Alicia into club dates, which Jeff felt that she was not ready for, he took the time to prepare her for a career.

After working with Alicia for six months, Jeff knew it was time to interest record labels. Meanwhile, Alicia proved that her ability at school went beyond music. She graduated valedictorian in 1996 from the Professional Performing Arts School. Her grades were the highest in her class.

Alicia was 16 years old, and she had an important decision to make. She had to choose between college and a career.

Alicia Cook changed her last name to Keys to reflect her love for the piano.

Columbia or Columbia?

*A*licia's amateur performances with girl group EmBishion had landed her a manager. Jeff Robinson worked with his new client to prepare her for the business as his brother Conrad made sure Alicia's voice was the best it could be. Instead of creating a standard demo tape, where a singer's voice is recorded and sent to record labels, Jeff took a different approach.

Six months after he signed her, Jeff set up a showcase for Alicia. This invitation-only performance would be a chance for record label executives to hear Alicia perform live.

On a bare stage, with just young Alicia, a microphone, and a piano, she was an instant hit. Immediately a number of representatives from major record labels wanted her to sign with them. A bidding war began. The labels competed against each other to see who would offer the most money and best perks.

Columbia Records won the war, offering a reported $400,000 deal to the teenager. Alicia had been studying music for more than half of her life. She had performed in talent shows and in small venues. She had worked hard to get this far. It seemed as though her future would be easy. In many ways, her struggle was just beginning.

> *Alicia had been studying music for half of her life. She had performed in talent shows and in small venues.*

Creating an album and working with the record company was harder than Alicia had imagined. No one seemed to take her seriously and she found herself being treated more like a kid than a recording artist. She began to feel depressed.

Meanwhile, the valedictorian accepted Columbia University's offer of a partial scholarship. She attended classes at the Ivy League college during the day. At night she worked on her debut album. It was too much pressure. The strain of trying to develop a record while being faithful to her studies was so stressful that Alicia dropped out of Columbia after less than a month.

Her situation at Columbia Records did not improve either.

With a few legal forms, Alicia Cook changed her name to Alicia Keys, a good fit for a piano player. Unfortunately, fitting in at Columbia Records was not so simple. Her manager, Jeff Robinson, realized that protecting his client's best interests was his number one concern; he pulled her out of the recording studio and helped Alicia, now 17, set up an apartment on 137th Street between Lenox and Fifth Avenue. It was a sixth floor walk-up, which means the building did not have an elevator. Moving to Harlem "was necessary for my sanity," Alicia later told *Rolling Stone*. "I needed to have my own thoughts, do my own thing."

Alicia did more than just leave her home. She left the overwhelming demands of the music producers she had been working with as well. Already familiar with a keyboard, it was a natural progression for Alicia to begin working with sound engineers at a mixing board. She installed recording equipment in her Harlem bedroom. She became her own producer.

Already familiar with a keyboard, it was a natural progression for Alicia to begin working with sound engineers at a mixing board.

Drawing on inspiration from her new neighborhood, Alicia began crafting the songs she had been working to create since signing with Columbia. It was a difficult process. When neighbors complained about the noise, she moved to New Jersey, and then the New York City borough of Queens. She continued to make regular trips to Harlem, and slowly built her album as her

Alicia accepts the award for Best Female R&B/Soul Album at the 2002 Soul Train Awards.

manager fended off executives from Columbia who worried that it was taking too long.

Finally, Alicia was done. The songs she had recorded were ones she believed in. She thought her efforts would be appreciated by the record label, but she was wrong. When Columbia Records executives heard Alicia's new music, they complained that it sounded like one long demo. They doubted that it would get airplay on the radio, which was very important for album sales. They wanted to add more beats, and create a danceable sound. Alicia was not happy about their demands. She felt that by giving in to the record company's wishes, she would lose her identity.

"They tried to tell me, 'we'll get you the top this and the top that and we'll get you a more radio friendly sound and we'll da-da-da-da,' " Alicia recalled for the *New York Times*. "But they had already set the monster loose. Once I started producing my own stuff, there wasn't any going back."

Alicia told her manager what she wanted. She asked for the album that she had labored on for the last two years of her life to be released as it was, sounding the way she wanted it to sound, not the way some older record executive believed it should sound. The work she had done represented Alicia's experiences and her poetry. It mirrored the life she had had growing up in places like Hell's Kitchen and Harlem. It was real, and she did not want someone else changing it.

> *Alicia told her manager what she wanted. She asked for the album that she labored on for the last two years of her life to be released . . .*

Jeff Robinson agreed with her. He realized in order for him to help make her dreams come true, she would have to get out of her contract with Columbia. There was only one problem. In order for that to happen, another label would have to pay Columbia back. That would take a lot of money.

J Records

*L*ike Alicia Keys, Clive Davis was raised in a lower middle class household surrounded by a difficult New York neighborhood. Hard work and focus helped Clive succeed just as it would for Alicia.

Clive Davis made it through Harvard Law School, and in 1956, became an attorney. However, the life of a lawyer, studying contracts, helping corporations, and planning estates grew boring. After a few years at several small firms, Clive was hired by CBS, which then owned Columbia Records and would later sign Alicia Keys.

Clive eventually became the president of Columbia, and discovered recording stars like Janis Joplin, Billy Joel, and Bruce Springsteen.

He was later fired by the record label. Although he was accused of stealing money from Columbia, the charges were never proven. Clive quickly overcame the difficult situation by founding his own company, Arista Records. Begun in 1974, it would eventually be acquired by larger label BMG Entertainment. By the late 1990s Arista alone was worth several billion dollars.

BMG executives asked Clive Davis to retire. He was 67 years old, but he was not ready to leave the music business for a life of leisure. Instead he convinced BMG to let him start a smaller record label. This new label would focus on just a few talented performers. In recent years, Clive had been responsible for launching the careers of artists as diverse as Sarah McLachlan and Sean "P. Diddy" Combs. He knew he could have just as much success with his own small label as he had with a large one. BMG agreed, and J Records was born.

Clive had watched Alicia perform at a Christmas showcase. He recognized that she was something special.

For Clive Davis, it was the second label he had launched. For Alicia Keys, it was a second chance.

As president of Arista, Clive had watched Alicia perform at a Christmas showcase. He recognized that she was something special. When he learned she was trying to get out of her contract with Columbia, he offered to bring her over to Arista, with

Clive Davis and Alicia Keys at the Clive Davis Pre-Grammy party held at the Beverly Hills Hotel.

the label paying back Columbia. "Did I know she was going to sell a million records? Of course not! I knew she was unique, I knew she was special," Clive told *Rolling Stone.* "I knew she was a self-contained artist. But did I know with Janis Joplin? Did I know with Springsteen? When you sign them, you don't know, so waiting for artistry to flower and giving them the space to do it is the thing."

Alicia's manager Jeff Robinson knew Clive had a great reputation in the music industry. But what mattered most to Alicia, was what he said to her when he signed her. "Just be yourself," Clive advised.

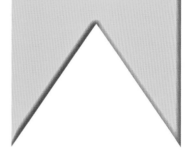

But what mattered most to Alicia, was what [Clive] said to her when he signed her. "Just be yourself," Clive advised.

Alicia could not be anything but herself. She signed with Arista in late 1998, and then moved with Clive to his new label, J Records, the next year. Unfortunately, the challenges of starting a new record label kept Clive from releasing Alicia's debut album. The waiting tested Alicia's confidence but helped her to prepare for what was about to come.

As Clive organized the release of Alicia's album, he realized the executives at Columbia had been right about one thing. Alicia Keys' music was very different from what was played on the radio. Clive did not expect stations to play any of the singles from Alicia's album, which would lead to automatic attention and a fan base. He needed to get her noticed before the album came out.

Once again, showcases made the difference. Alicia performed her songs before a number of well-connected people, including a talent scout for the *Tonight Show*. He immediately booked her on the program, despite the fact that her album had not yet been released.

Clive Davis also wrote a letter to Oprah Winfrey, saying, "What you've done with books is well-known. In music, you play established artists. How about new women in music? Why don't you put on Jill Scott, India Arie, and Alicia Keys, my artist without an album?"

Clive received a call as soon as the Oprah staff opened his letter, and Alicia was booked for the show.

Alicia's appearances on the *Tonight Show* and *Oprah Winfrey*, along with regular airplay on MTV for her single "Fallin'," earned her numerous fans. Clive's strategy worked. By the time Alicia Keys' album, *Songs in A Minor* came out, thousands of people knew who she was and wanted to buy the CD. Released in June of 2001, *Songs in A Minor* became the number one selling album in the country. Alicia was finally a star.

Alicia Keys performs on stage at the 2004 Black Entertainment Awards held at the Kodak Theatre in Hollywood.

Awards and Rewards

*A*licia Keys' debut album would sell over four million copies before 2001 ended. She went from being an unknown artist to an opening act to a headliner in less than a year. By the spring of 2002, she was preparing for a summer tour. But one thing bothered her. People assumed she was an overnight success because they had never heard of her before. No one realized how hard Alicia had worked over the years to get where she was.

She also realized that just as some had tried to manipulate her music, others might try to alter her image. She was young, attractive, and had a face and body designed for magazine covers. Alicia did not mind the attention, but she knew her looks were not the most important part of what she had to offer.

"There's so many stereotypes and lines drawn, especially for women, as I see the more I grow," Alicia

Alicia poses backstage with Stevie Wonder and Lenny Kravitz at the 2004 MTV Video Music Awards.

explained recently in a New York Times interview. "And maybe you change every day. . . . I'm definitely not one to look at people and judge them, but I do know we have to raise the standard. I think about who is going to be in my audience and how it is going to affect them. I'm 20, so I'm on a certain level. But at the same time, there are people in my audience who are 11, 12. They're looking at me as what is cool or what they should be like. It's something that I have to be conscious of, and I don't mind being conscious of it. But first and foremost I have to come from the place within, and make sure that I love it and that it means something to me."

She admitted to *Billboard* magazine, "Even though I've heard songs about it, I never realized how universal music is . . . and how much it makes us connect." Alicia connected with fans across the world as global sales of her debut album topped eight million by 2002. She was also the main reason for the success of Clive Davis's new label J Records. In its first year the label would have sales of $200 million. Yet while Davis' experience in the industry helped Alicia succeed, he also realized that talent like Alicia's was going to get noticed no matter who was backing her. "People talk about what I did for Alicia," he told *Variety*, " but I can only do it for Alicia because she did it for herself. If you put her in Joe's Pub with a piano and a microphone she will mesmerize you."

> *Alicia connected with fans across the world as global sales of her debut album topped eight million by 2002.*

Alicia's success in 2001 and early 2002 was not just about album sales. Critics applauded her debut effort. She received prizes from MTV the American Music Awards, Billboard, and Soul Train. The trophies and other honors probably would have filled her old apartment in Harlem. Still, Alicia knew in the music industry, it is the Grammy Award that is seen by many as the pinnacle in a recording artist's climb to the top. Alicia Keys was nominated for six Grammys.

Alicia wins Best R&B Video at the 2004 MTV Video Music Awards.

On February 28, 2002, in a ceremony held at the Los Angeles Staples Center, Alicia took home five of the awards.

It has been a long road from Hell's Kitchen and Harlem to the Grammy Awards, but Alicia managed to do it her own way.

Over the next several years, Alicia toured the world singing to sold-out crowds. She visited China and Australia; won many more awards, and in 2003, released her second album, *The Diary of Alicia Keys*. In September 2004, Alicia was nominated for the American Music Awards for both Soul R&B Favorite Female Artist and Soul R&B Favorite Album for *The Diary of Alicia Keys*.

It has been a long road from Hell's Kitchen and Harlem to the Grammy Awards, but Alicia managed to do it her own way: by believing in herself, trusting in her music, and never giving up.

DISCOGRAPHY

Albums
2003   *The Diary of Alicia Keys*
2001   *Songs in A Minor*

Singles
2004   "Karma"
        "If I Ain't Got You"
2003   "You Don't Know My Name"
        "Gangsta Love" (with Eve)
2002   "How Come You Don't Call Me"
2001   "A Woman's Worth"
        "Fallin' "
        "Girlfriend"
        "What's Goin On"

Other Songs/Tributes by Alicia
        "Dah Dee Dah (Sexy Thing)" from *Men in Black*
        "Rock Wit U" from *Shaft*
        "Fight" from *Ali*
        "Little Drummer Girl" from *So So Def Christmas*
        "Someday We'll All Be Free" from *America: A Tribute to Heroes Benefit*

Awards
2004   Best R&B Video Award for "If I Ain't Got You"; NAACP Image Award for Best Female Artist
2002   American Music Awards for "Best New Artist" and "Favorite New Female R&B Star Artist"
        Grammy Awards (five) including "Song of the Year" (for "Fallin'") and "Best New Artist"
        Soul Train Awards for "Best R&B/Soul or Rap New Artist" and "Best R&B/Soul Female Album"
2001   MTV Video Music Award for "Best New Artist Video"
        BillBoard Music Awards for "Female New Artist of the Year" and "New R&B/Hip-Hop Artist"

CHRONOLOGY

1981   Alicia Augello Cook is born on January 25 in New York, New York

1985   Wins the lead role in a kindergarten production of the *Wizard of Oz*

1988   Begins studying piano

1993   Accepted to the Professional Performing Arts Scool

1996   Graduates valedictorian; offered scholarship to attend Columbia University, signs with Columbia Records

1998   Released from Columbia; signs with Arista

1999   Leaves Arista for J Records

2001   Debut album, *Songs in A Minor* is released and is ranked number one

2002   Wins five Grammmy awards

2003   The album *The Diary of Alicia Keys* reaches #1 on the Billboard album charts; sings with Eve in her song "Gangsta Love"

2004   *The Diary of Alicia Keys* becomes a triple platinum album; sings with Usher in his song "My Boo"; wins Best R&B Video for "If I Ain't Got You" at the 2004 MTV Video Music Awards; wins songwriter of the year at the African American Literary Awards; wins NAACP Award for Best Female Artist

FOR FURTHER READING

Books

Graham, Ben. *Maximum Alicia Keys: The Unauthorised Biography of Alicia Keys*. Chrome Dreams, Abridged Edition, 2003.

Keys, Alicia. *Tears for Water: Songbook of Poem and Lyrics*. Putnam Publishing, 2004.

Websites

Alicia Keys—www.aliciakeys.net

Alicia Keys Fan—www.aliciakeysfan.com

Alicia Keys co.uk—www.aliciakeys.co.uk

MTV.com - Alicia Keys—www.mtv.com/bands/az/keys_alicia/news.jhtml

INDEX